# Color

# Color
## Countee Cullen

MINT EDITIONS

*Color* was first published in 1925.

This edition published by Mint Editions 2021.

ISBN 9781513282381 | E-ISBN 9781513287409

Published by Mint Editions®

minteditionbooks.com

Publishing Director: Jennifer Newens
Design & Production: Rachel Lopez Metzger
Project Manager: Micaela Clark
Typesetting: Westchester Publishing Services

# Contents

For Love's Sake

Varia

# To You Who Read My Book

Soon every sprinter,
However feet,
Comes to a winter
Of sure defeat:
Though he may race
Like the hunted doe,
Time has a pace
To lay him low.

Soon we who sing,
However high,
Must face the Thing
We cannot fly.
Yea, though we fling
Our notes to the sun,
Time will outsing
Us every one.

All things must change
As the wind is blown;
Time will estrange
The flesh from the bone.

The dream shall elude
The dreamer's clasp,
And only its hood
Shall comfort his grasp.

A little while,
Too brief at most,
And even my smile
Will be a ghost.
A little space,
A Finger's crook,
And who shall trace
The path I took?

Who shall declare
My whereabouts;
Say if in the air
My being shouts
Along light ways,
Or if in the sea,
Or deep earth stays
The germ of me?

Ah, none knows, none,
Save (but too well)
The Cryptic One
Who will not tell.

This is my hour
To wax and climb,
Flaunt a red flower
In the face of time.
And only an hour
Time gives, then snap
Goes the flower,
And dried is the sap.

Juice of the first
Grapes of my vine,
I proffer your thirst
My own heart's wine.
Here of my growing
A red rose sways,
Seed of my sowing,
And work of my days.

(I run, but time's
Abreast with me;
I sing, but he climbs
With my highest C.)

Drink while my blood
Colors the wine,

Reach while the bud
Is still on the vine. . .

Then. . . .
When the hawks of death
Tear at my throat
Till song and breath
Ebb note by note,
Turn to this book
Of the mellow word
For a singing look
At the stricken bird.

Say, "This is the way
He chirped and sung,
In the sweet heyday
When his heart was young.
Though his throat is bare,
By death defiled,
Song labored there
And bore a child."

When the dreadful Ax
Rives me apart
When the sharp wedge cracks
My arid heart,
Turn to this book
Of the singing me
For a springtime look
At the wintry tree.

Say, "Thus it was weighed
With flower and fruit,
Ere the Ax was laid
Unto its root.
Though the blows fall free
On a gnarled trunk now,
Once he was a tree
With a blossomy bough."

COLOR

# Yet Do I Marvel

I Doubt not God is good, well-meaning, kind,
And did He stoop to quibble could tell why
The little buried mole continues blind,
Why flesh that mirrors Him must some day die,
Make plain the reason tortured Tantalus
Is baited by the fickle fruit, declare
If merely brute caprice dooms Sisyphus
To struggle up a never-ending stair.
Inscrutable His ways are, and immune
To catechism by a mind too strewn
With petty cares to slightly understand
What awful brain compels His awful hand.
Yet do I marvel at this curious thing:
To make a poet black, and bid him sing!

# A Song of Praise

(For one who praised his lady's being fair.)

You have not heard my love's dark throat,
Slow-fluting like a reed,
Release the perfect golden note
She caged there for my need.

Her walk is like the replica
Of some barbaric dance
Wherein the soul of Africa
Is winged with arrogance.

And yet so light she steps across
The ways her sure feet pass,
She does not dent the smoothest moss
Or bend the thinnest grass.

My love is dark as yours is fair,
Yet lovelier I hold her
Than listless maids with pallid hair,
And blood that's thin and colder.

You-proud-and-to-be-pitied one,
Gaze on her and despair;
Then seal your lips until the sun
Discovers one as fair.

# Brown Boy to Brown Girl

### (Remembrance on a hill) (For Yolande)

"As surely as I hold your hand in mine,
As surely as your crinkled hair belies
The enamoured sun pretending that he dies
While still he loiters in its glossy shine,
As surely as I break the slender line
That spider linked us with, in no least wise
Am I uncertain that these alien skies
Do not our whole life measure and confine.
No less, once in a land of scarlet suns
And brooding winds, before the hurricane
Bore down upon us, long before this pain,
We found a place where quiet water runs;
I held your hand this way upon a hill,
And felt my heart forebear, my pulse grow

# A Brown Girl Dead

With two white roses on her breasts,
White candles at head and feet,
Dark Madonna of the grave she rests;
Lord Death has found her sweet.

Her mother pawned her wedding ring
To lay her out in white;
She'd be so proud she'd dance and sing
To see herself tonight.

# To a Brown Girl

## (For Roberta)

What if his glance is bold and free,
His mouth the lash of whips?
So should the eyes of lovers be,
And so a lover's lips.

What if no puritanic strain
Confines him to the nice?
He will not pass this way again,
Nor hunger for you twice.

Since in the end consort together
Magdalen and Mary,
Youth is the time for careless weather:
Later, lass, be wary.

# To a Brown Boy

That brown girl's swagger gives a twitch
To beauty like a queen;
Lad, never dam your body's itch
When loveliness is seen.

For there is ample room for bliss
In pride in clean, brown limbs,
And lips know better how to kiss
Than how to raise white hymns.

And when your body's death gives birth
To soil for spring to crown,
Men will not ask if that rare earth
Was white flesh once, or brown.

# Black Magdalens

These have no Christ to spit and stoop
To write upon the sand,
Inviting him that has not sinned
To raise the first rude hand.

And if he came they could not buy
Rich ointment for his feet,
The body's sale scarce yields enough
To let the body eat.

The chaste clean ladies pass them by
And draw their skirts aside,
But Magdalens have a ready laugh;
They wrap their wounds in pride.

They fare full ill since Christ forsook
The cross to mount a throne,
And Virtue still is stooping down
To cast the first hard stone.

# ATLANTIC CITY WAITER

With subtle poise he grips his tray
Of delicate things to eat;
Choice viands to their mouths half way,
The ladies watch his feet

Go carving dexterous avenues
Through sly intricacies;
Ten thousand years on jungle clues
Alone shaped feet like these.

For him to be humble who is proud
Needs colder artifice;
Though half his pride is disavowed,
In vain the sacrifice.

Sheer through his acquiescent mask
Of bland gentility,
The jungle flames like a copper cask
Set where the sun strikes free.

# Near White

Ambiguous of race they stand,
By one disowned, scorned of another,
Not knowing where to stretch a hand,
And cry, "My sister" or "My brother."

# Tableau

### For Donald Duff

Locked arm in arm they cross the way,
The black boy and the white,
The golden splendor of the day,
The sable pride of night.

From lowered blinds the dark folk stare,
And here the fair folk talk,
Indignant that these two should dare
In unison to walk.

Oblivious to look and word
They pass, and see no wonder
That lightning brilliant as a sword
Should blaze the path of thunder.

# Harlem Wine

This is not water running here,
These thick rebellious streams
That hurtle flesh and bone past fear
Down alleyways of dreams.

This is a wine that must flow on
Not caring how nor where,
So it has ways to flow upon
Where song is in the air.

So it can woo an artful flute
With loose, elastic lips,
Its measurement of joy compute
With blithe, ecstatic hips.

# Simon the Cyrenian Speaks

He never spoke a word to me,
And yet He called my name;
He never gave a sign to me,
And yet I knew and came.

At first I said, "I will not bear
His cross upon my back;
He only seeks to place it there
Because my skin is black."

But He was dying for a dream,
And He was very meek,
And in His eyes there shone a gleam
Men journey far to seek.

It was Himself my pity bought;
I did for Christ alone What all of Rome could not have wrought
With bruise of lash or stone.

# INCIDENT

### (For Eric Walrond)

Once riding in old Baltimore,
Heart-filled, head-filled with glee,
I saw a Baltimorean
Keep looking straight at me.

Now I was eight and very small,
And he was no whit bigger,
And so I smiled, but he poked out
His tongue, and called me, "Nigger.".

I saw the whole of Baltimore
From May until December;
Of all the things that happened there
That's all that I remember.

# Two Who Crossed a Line

## (She Crosses)

From where she stood the air she craved
Smote with the smell of pine;
It was too much to bear; she braved
Her gods and crossed the line.

And we were hurt to see her go,
With her fair face and hair,
And veins too thin and blue to show
What mingled blood flowed there.

We envied her a while, who still
Pursued the hated track;
Then we forgot her name, until
One day her shade came back.

Calm as a wave without a crest,
Sorrow-proud and sorrow-wise,
With trouble sucking at her breast,
With tear-disdainful eyes,

She slipped into her ancient place,
And, no word asked, gave none;
Only the silence in her face
Said seats were dear in the sun.

# Two Who Crossed a Line

## (He Crosses)

He rode across like a cavalier,
Spurs clicking hard and loud;
And where he tarried dropped his tear
On heads he left low-bowed.

But, "Even Stephen," he cried, and struck
His steed an urgent blow;
He swore by youth he was a buck
With savage oats to sow.

To even up some standing scores,
From every flower bed He passed,
He plucked by threes and fours
Till wheels whirled in his head.

But long before the drug could tell,
He took his anodyne;
With scornful grace, he bowed farewell
And retraversed the line.

# SATURDAY'S CHILD

Come are teethed on a silver spoon,
With the stars strung for a rattle;
I cut my teeth as the black raccoon-
For implements of battle.

Some are swaddled in silk and down,
And heralded by a star;
They swathed my limbs in a sackcloth gown
On a night that was black as tar.

For some, godfather and goddame
The opulent fairies be;
Dame Poverty gave me my name,
And Pain godfathered me.

For I was born on Saturday,
"Bad time for planting a seed,"
Was all my father had to say,
And, "One mouth more to feed."

Death cut the strings that gave me life,
And handed me to Sorrow,
The only kind of middle wife
My folks could beg or borrow.

# The Dance of Love

### (After reading René Maran's "Batouala")

All night we danced upon our windy hill,
Your dress a cloud of tangled midnight hair,
And love was much too much for me to wear
My leaves; the killer roared above his kill,
But you danced on, and when some star would spill
Its red and white upon you whirling there,
I sensed a hidden beauty in the air;
Though you danced on, my heart and I stood still.

But suddenly a bit of morning crept
Along your trembling sides of ebony;
I saw the tears your tired limbs had wept,
And how your breasts heaved high, how languidly
Your dark arms moved; I drew you close to me;
We flung ourselves upon our hill and slept.

# PAGAN PRAYER

Not for myself I make this prayer,
But for this race of mine
That stretches forth from shadowed places
Dark hands for bread and wine.

For me, my heart is pagan mad,
My feet are never still,
But give them hearths to keep them warm
In homes high on a hill.

For me, my faith lies fallowing,
I bow not till I see,
But these are humble and believe;
Bless their credulity.

For me, I pay my debts in kind,
And see no better way,
Bless these who turn the other cheek
For love of you, and pray.

Our Father, God, our Brother, Christ
So are we taught to pray;
Their kinship seems a little thing
Who sorrow all the day.

Our Father, God; our Brother, Christ,
Or are we bastard kin,
That to our plaints your ears are closed,
Your doors barred from within?

Our Father, God; our Brother, Christ,
Retrieve my race again;
So shall you compass this black'sheep,
This pagan heart. Amen.

# Wisdom Cometh With the Years

Now I am young and credulous,
My heart is quick to bleed
At courage in the tremulous
Slow sprouting of a seed.

Now I am young and sensitive,
Man's lack can stab me through;
I own no stitch I would not give
To him that asked me to.

Now I am young and a fool for love,
My blood goes mad to see
A brown girl pass me like a dove
That flies melodiously.

Let me be lavish of my tears,
And dream that false is true;
Though wisdom cometh with the years,
The barren days come, too.

# To My Fairer Brethren

Though I score you with my best,
Treble circumstance
Must confirm the verdict, lest
It be laid to chance.

Insufficient that I match you
Every coin you flip;
Your demand is that I catch you
Squarely on the hip.

Should I wear my wreaths a bit
Rakishly and proud,
I have bought my right to it;
Let it be allowed.

# Fruit of the Flower

My father is a quiet man
With sober, steady ways;
For simile, a folded fan;
His nights are like his days.

My mother's life is puritan,
No hint of cavalier,
A pool so calm you're sure it can
Have little depth to fear.

And yet my father's eyes can boast
How full his life has been;
There haunts them yet the languid ghost
Of some still sacred sin.

And though my mother chants of God,
And of the mystic river,
I've seen a bit of checkered sod
Set all her flesh aquiver.

Why should he deem it pure mischance
A son of his is fain
To do a naked tribal dance
Each time he hears the rain?

Why should she think it devil's art
That all my songs should be
Of love and lovers, broken heart,
And wild sweet agony?

Who plants a seed begets a bud,
Extract of that same root;
Why marvel at the hectic blood
That flushes this wild fruit?

# The Shroud of Color

## (For Llewellyn Ransom)

"Lord, being dark," I said, "I cannot
  bear The further touch of earth, the scented air;
Lord, being dark, forewilled to that despair
My color shrouds me in, I am as dirt
Beneath my brother's heel; there is a hurt
In all the simple joys which to a child
Are sweet; they are contaminate, defiled
By truths of wrongs the childish vision fails
To see; too great a cost this birth entails.
I strangle in this yoke drawn tighter than
The worth of bearing it, just to be man.
I am not brave enough to pay the price
In full; I lack the strength to sacrifice.
I who have burned my hands upon a star,
And climbed high hills at dawn to view the far
Illimitable wonderments of earth,
For whom all cups have dripped the wine of mirth,
For whom the sea. has strained her honeyed throat
Till all the world was sea, and I a boat
Unmoored, on what strange quest I willed to float;
Who wore a many-colored coat of dreams,
Thy gift, O Lord—I whom sun-dabbled streams
Have washed, whose bare brown thighs have held
   the sun
Incarcerate until his course was run,
I who considered man a high-perfected
Glass where loveliness could lie reflected,
Now that I sway athwart Truth's deep abyss,
Denuding man for what he was and is,
Shall breath and being so inveigle me
That I can damn my dreams to hell, and be
Content, each new-born day, anew to see
The steaming crimson vintage of my youth
Incarnadine the altar-slab of Truth?

Or hast Thou, Lord, somewhere I cannot see,
A lamb imprisoned in a bush for me?

Not so? Then let me render one by one
Thy gifts, while still they shine; some little sun
Yet gilds these thighs; my coat, albeit worn,
Still holds its colors fast; albeit torn,
My heart will laugh a little yet, if I
May win of Thee this grace, Lord: on this high
And sacrificial hill 'twixt earth and sky,
To dream still pure all that I loved, and die.
There is no other way to keep secure
My wild chimeras; grave-locked against the lure
Of Truth, the small hard teeth of worms, yet less
Envenomed than the mouth of Truth, will bless
Them into dust and happy nothingness.
Lord, Thou art God; and I, Lord, what am I
But dust? With dust my place. Lord, let me die."

Across the earth's warm, palpitating crust
I flung my body in embrace; I thrust
My mouth into the grass and sucked the dew,
Then gave it back in tears my anguish drew;
So hard I pressed against the ground, I felt
The smallest sandgrain like a knife, and smelt
The next year's flowering; all this to speed
My body's dissolution, fain to feed
The worms. And so I groaned, and spent my strength

Until, all passion spent, I lay full length
And quivered like a flayed and bleeding thing.

So lay till lifted on a great black wing
That had no mate nor flesh-apparent trunk
To hamper it; with me all time had sunk
Into oblivion; when I awoke
The wing hung poised above two cliffs that broke
The bowels of the earth in twain, and cleft
The seas apart. Below, above, to left,

To right, I saw what no man saw before:
Earth, hell, and heaven; sinew, vein, and core.
All things that swim or walk or creep or fly,
All things that live and hunger, faint and die,
Were made majestic then and magnified
By sight so clearly purged and deified.
The smallest bug that crawls was taller than
A tree, the mustard seed loomed like a man.
The earth that writhes eternally with pain
Of birth, and woe of taking back her slain,
Laid bare her teeming bosom to my sight,
And all was struggle, gasping breath, and fight.
A blind worm here dug tunnels to the light,
And there a seed, racked with heroic pain,
Thrust eager tentacles to sun and rain;

It climbed ; it died; the old love conquered me
To weep the blossom it would never be.
But here a bud won light; it burst and flowered
Into a rose whose beauty challenged, "Coward!"
There was no thing alive save only I
That held life in contempt and longed to die.
And still I writhed and moaned, "The curse, the curse,
Than animated death, can death be worse?"

*"Dark child of sorrow, mine no less, what art*
*Of mine can make thee see and play thy part?*
*The key to all strange things is in thy heart."*

What voice was this that coursed like liquid fire
Along my flesh, and turned my hair to wire?

I raised my burning eyes, beheld a field
All multitudinous with carnal yield,
A grim ensanguined mead whereon I saw
Evolve the ancient fundamental law
Of tooth and talon, fist and nail and claw.
There with the force of living, hostile hills

Whose clash the hemmed-in vale with clamor fills,
With greater din contended fierce majestic wills
Of beast with beast, of man with man, in strife
For love of what my heart despised, for life
That unto me at dawn was now a prayer
For night, at night a bloody heart-wrung tear
For day again; for *this*, these groans
From tangled flesh and interlocked bones.
And no thing died that did not give A testimony that it longed to live.
Man, strange composite blend of brute and god,
Pushed on, nor backward glanced where last he trod.
He seemed to mount a misty ladder flung
Pendant from a cloud, yet never gained a rung
But at his feet another tugged and clung.
My heart was still a pool of bitterness,
Would yield nought else, nought else confess.
I spoke (although no form was there
To see, I knew an ear was there to hear),
"Well, let them fight; they *can* whose flesh is fair."

Crisp lightning flashed; a wave of thunder shook
My wing; a pause, and then a speaking, "Look."
I scarce dared trust my ears or eyes for awe
Of what they heard, and dread of what they saw;
For, privileged beyond degree, this flesh
Beheld God and His heaven in the mesh
Of Lucifer's revolt, saw Lucifer
Glow like the sun, and like a dulcimer
I heard his sin-sweet voice break on the yell
Of God's great warriors: Gabriel,
Saint Clair and Michael, Israfel and Raphael.
And strange it was to see God with His back
Against a wall, to see Christ hew and hack
Till Lucifer, pressed by the mighty pair,
And losing inch by inch, clawed at the air
With fevered wings; then, lost beyond repair,
He tricked a mass of stars into his hair;
He filled his hands with stars, crying as he fell,

"A star's a star although it burns in hell."
So God was left to His divinity,
Omnipotent at that most costly fee.

There was a lesson here, but still the clod
In me was sycophant unto the rod,
And cried, "Why mock me thus? Am I a god?"

*"One trial more: this failing, then I give*
*You leave to die; no further need to live."*

Now suddenly a strange wild music smote
A chord long impotent in me; a note
Of jungles, primitive and subtle, throbbed
Against my echoing breast, and tom-toms sobbed
In every pulse-beat of my frame. The din
A hollow log bound with a python's skin
Can make wrought every nerve to ecstasy,
And I was wind and sky again, and sea,
And all sweet things that flourish, being free.

Till all at once the music changed its key.

And now it was of bitterness and death,
The cry the lash extorts, the broken breath
Of liberty enchained; and yet there ran
Through all a harmony. of faith in man,
A knowledge all would end as it began.
All sights and sounds and aspects of my race
Accompanied this melody, kept pace
With it; with music all their hopes and hates
Were charged, not to be downed by all the fates.
And somehow it was borne upon my brain
How being dark, and living through the pain
Of it, is courage more than angels have. I knew
What storms and tumults lashed the tree that grew
This body that I was, this cringing I
That feared to contemplate a changing sky,
This that I grovelled, whining, "Let me die,"

While others struggled in Life's abattoir.
The cries of all dark people near or far
Were billowed over me, a mighty surge
Of suffering in which my puny grief must merge
And lose itself; I had no further claim to urge
For death; in shame I raised my dust-grimed head,
And though my lips moved not, God knew I said,
"Lord, not for what I saw in flesh or bone
Of fairer men; not raised on faith alone;
Lord, I will live persuaded by mine own.
I cannot play the recreant to these;
My spirit has come home, that sailed the doubtful seas."
With the whiz of a sword that severs space,
The wing dropped down at a dizzy pace,
And flung me on my hill flat on my face;
Flat on my face I lay defying pain,
Glad of the blood in my smallest vein,
And in my hands I clutched a loyal dream,
Still spitting fire, bright twist and coil and gleam,
And chiselled like a hound's white tooth.
"Oh, I will match you yet," I cried, "to truth."

Right glad I was to stoop to what I once had spurned,
Glad even unto tears; I laughed aloud; I turned
Upon my back, and though the tears for joy would run,
My sight was clear; I looked and saw the rising sun.

# HERITAGE

## (For Harold Jackman)

What is Africa to me:
Copper sun or scarlet sea,
Jungle star or jungle track,
Strong bronzed men, or regal black
Women from whose loins I sprang
When the birds of Eden sang?
*One three centuries removed*
*From the scenes his fathers loved,*
*Spicy grove, cinnamon tree,*
*What is Africa to me?*

So I lie, who all day long
Want no sound except the song
Sung by wild barbaric birds
Goading massive jungle herds,
Juggernauts of flesh that pass
Trampling tall defiant grass
Where young forest lovers lie,
Plighting troth beneath the sky.
So I lie, who always hear,
Though I cram against my ear
Both my thumbs, and keep them there,
Great drums throbbing through the air.
So I lie, whose fount of pride,
Dear distress, and joy allied,
Is my somber flesh and skin,
With the dark blood dammed within
Like great pulsing tides of wine
That, I fear, must burst the fine
Channels of the chafing net
Where they surge and foam and fret.

Africa? A book one thumbs
Listlessly, till slumber comes.

Unremembered are her bats
Circling through the night, her cats
Crouching in the river reeds,
Stalking gentle flesh that feeds
By the river brink; no more
Does the bugle-throated roar
Cry that monarch claws have leapt
From the scabbards where they slept.
Silver snakes that once a year
Doff the lovely coats you wear,
Seek no covert in your fear
Lest a mortal eye should see;
What's your nakedness to me?
Here no leprous flowers rear
Fierce corollas in the air;

Here no bodies sleek and wet,
Dripping mingled rain and sweat,
Tread the savage measures of
Jungle boys and girls in love.
What is last year's snow to me,
Last year's anything? The tree
Budding yearly must forget
How its past arose or set—
Bough and blossom, flower, fruit,
Even what shy bird with mute
Wonder at her travail there,
Meekly labored in its hair.
*One three centuries removed*
*From the scenes his fathers loved,*
*Spicy grove, cinnamon tree,*
*What is Africa to me?*

So I lie, who find no peace
Night or day, no slight release
From the unremittant beat
Made by cruel padded feet
Walking through my body's street.
Up and down they go, and back,

Treading out a jungle track.
So I lie, who never quite
Safely sleep from rain at night-
I can never rest at all

When the rain begins to fall;
Like a soul gone mad with pain
I must match its weird refrain;
Ever must I twist and squirm,
Writhing like a baited worm,
While its primal measures drip
Through my body, crying, "Strip!
Doff this new exuberance.
Come and dance the Lover's Dance!"
In an old remembered way
Rain works on me night and day.

Quaint, outlandish heathen gods
Black men fashion out of rods,
Clay, and brittle bits of stone,
In a likeness like their own,
My conversion came high-priced;
I belong to Jesus Christ,
Preacher of humility;
Heathen gods are naught to me.

Father, Son, and Holy Ghost,
So I make an idle boast;
Jesus of the twice-turned cheek,
Lamb of God, although I speak
With my mouth thus, in my heart
Do I play a double part.

Ever at Thy glowing altar
Must my heart grow sick and falter,
Wishing He I served were black,
Thinking then it would not lack
Precedent of pain to guide it,
Let who would or might deride it;

Surely then this flesh would know
Yours had borne a kindred woe.
Lord, I fashion dark gods, too,
Daring even to give You
Dark despairing features where,
Crowned with dark rebellious hair,
Patience wavers just so much as
Mortal grief compels, while touches
Quick and hot, of anger, rise
To smitten cheek and weary eyes.
Lord, forgive me if my need
Sometimes shapes a human creed.

*All day long and all night through,*
*One thing only must I do:*
*Quench my pride and cool my blood,*
*Lest I perish in the flood.*
*Lest a hidden ember set*
*Timber that I thought was wet*
*Burning like the dryest flax,*

*Melting like the merest wax,*
*Lest the grave restore its dead.*
*Not yet has my heart or head*
*In the least way realized*
*They and I are civilized.*

EPITAPHS

# For a Poet

### (To John Gaston Edgar)

I Have wrapped my dreams in a silken cloth,
And laid them away in a box of gold:
Where long will cling the lips of the moth,
I have wrapped my dreams in a silken cloth;
I hide no hate; I am not even wroth
Who found earth's breath so keen and cold;
I have wrapped my dreams in a silken cloth,
And laid them away in a box of gold.

# For My Grandmother

This lovely flower fell to seed;
Work gently, sun and rain;
She held it as her dying creed
That she would grow again.

# For a Cynic

Birth is a crime
All men commit;
Life gives them time
To atone for it;
Death ends the rhyme
As the price for it.

# For a Singer

Death clogged this flute
At its highest note;
Song sleeps here mute
In this breathless throat.

# For a Virgin

Ror forty years I shunned the lust
Inherent in my clay;
Death only was so amorous
I let him have his way.

# For a Lady I Know

She even thinks that up in heaven
Her class lies late and snores,
While poor black cherubs rise at seven
To do celestial chores.

# For a Lovely Lady

A Creature slender as a reed,
And sad-eyed as a doe Lies here (but take my word for it,
And do not pry below).

# For an Atheist

Mountains cover me like rain,
Billows whirl and rise;
Hide me from the stabbing pain
In His reproachful eyes.

# FOR AN EVOLUTIONIST
## AND HIS OPPONENT

Showing that our ways agreed,
Death is proof enough;
Body seeks the primal clay,
Soul transcends the slough.

# For an Anarchist

What matters that I stormed and swore?
Not Samson with an ass's jaw,
Not though a forest of hair he wore,
Could break death's adamantine law.

# For a Magician

I Whose magic could explore
Ways others might not guess or see,
Now am barred behind a door
That has no "Open Sesame."

# For a Pessimist

He wore his coffin for a hat,
Calamity his cape,
While on his face a death's-head sat
And waved a bit of crape.

## FOR A MOUTHY WOMAN

God and the devil still are wrangling
Which should have her, which repel;
God wants no discord in his heaven;
Satan has enough in hell.

# FOR A PHILOSOPHER

Here lies one who tried to solve
The riddle of being and breath:
The wee blind mole that gnaws his bones
Tells him the answer is death.

# For an Unsuccessful Sinner

I Boasted my sins were sure to sink me
Out of all sound and sight of glory;
And the most I've won for all my pains
Is a century of purgatory.

# For a Fool

On earth the wise man makes the rules,
And is the fool's adviser,
But here the wise are as the fools,
(And no man is the wiser).

# For One Who Gayly Sowed His Oats

My days were a thing for me to live,
For others to deplore;
I took of life all it could give:
Rind, inner fruit, and core.

# For a Skeptic

Blood-Brother unto Thomas whose
Weak faith doubt kept in trammels,
His little credence strained at gnats—
But grew robust on camels.

## For a Fatalist

Life ushers some as heirs-elect
To weather wind and gale;
Here lies a man whose ships were wrecked
Ere he could hoist a sail.

# For Daughters of Magdalen

Ours is the ancient story:
Delicate flowers of sin,
Lilies, arrayed in glory,
That would not toil nor spin.

# For a Wanton

To men no more than so much cover
For them to doff or try,
I found in Death a constant lover:
Here in his arms I lie.

# For a Preacher

Vanity of vanities,
All is vanity; yea,
Even the rod He flayed you with
Crumbled and turned to clay.

# For One Who Died Singing of Death

He whose might you sang so well
Living, will not let you rust:
Death has set the golden bell
Pealing in the courts of dust.

# For John Keats, Apostle of Beauty

Not writ in water, nor in mist,
Sweet lyric throat, thy name;
Thy singing lips that cold death kissed
Have seared his own with flame.

# For Hazel Hall, American Poet

Soul-Troubled at the febrile ways of breath,
 Her timid breast shot through with faint alarm,
"Yes, I'm a stranger here," she said to Death,
"It's kind of you to let me take your arm."

# For Paul Laurence Dunbar

Born of the sorrowful of heart,
Mirth was a crown upon his head;
Pride kept his twisted lips apart
In jest, to hide a heart that bled.

# For Joseph Conrad

Not of the dust, but of the wave
His final couch should be; They lie not easy in a grave
Who once have known the sea.
How shall earth's meagre bed enthrall
The hardiest seaman of them all?

# FOR MYSELF

What's in this grave is worth your tear;
There's more than the eye can see;
Folly and Pride and Love lie here
Buried alive with me.

# All the Dead

Priest and layman, virgin, strumpet,
Good and ill commingled sleep,
Waiting till the dreadful trumpet
Separates the wolves and sheep.

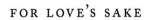

FOR LOVE'S SAKE

# OH, FOR A LITTLE WHILE BE KIND

## (For Ruth Marie)

Oh, for a little while be kind to me
Who stand in such imperious need of you,
And for a fitful space let my head lie
Happily on your passion's frigid breast.
Although yourself no more resigned to me
Than on all bitter yesterdays I knew,
This half a loaf from sumptuous crumbs your shy
Reneging hand lets fall shall make me blest.
The sturdy homage of a love that throws
Its strength about you, dawn and dusk, at bed
And board, is not for scorn. When all is said
With final amen certitude, who knows
But Dives found a matchless fragrance fled
When Lazarus no longer shocked his nose?

# If You Should Go

Love, leave me like the light,
The gently passing day;
We would not know, but for the night,
When it has slipped away.

Go quietly; a dream,
When done, should leave no trace
That it has lived, except a gleam
Across the dreamer's face

# To One Who Said Me Nay

This much the gods vouchsafe today:
That we two lie in the clover,
Watching the heavens dip and sway,
With galleons sailing over.

This much is granted for an hour :
That we are young and tender,
That I am bee and you are flower,
Honey-mouthed and swaying slender.

This sweet of sweets is ours now:
To wander through the land,
Plucking an apple from its bough
To toss from hand to hand.

No thing is certain, joy nor sorrow,
Except the hour we know it;
Oh, wear my heart today; tomorrow
Who knows where the winds will blow it?

# ADVICE TO YOUTH

## (For Guillaume)

Since little time is granted here
For pride in pain or play,
Since blood soon cools before that Fear
That makes our prowess clay,
If lips to kiss are freely met,
Lad, be not proud nor shy;
There are no lips where men forget,
And undesiring lie.

# Caprice

"I'll tell him, when he comes," she said,
"Body and baggage, to go,
 Though the night be darker than my hair,
 And the ground be hard with snow."

 But when he came with his gay black head
 Thrown back, and his lips apart,
 She flipped a light hair from his coat,
 And sobbed against his heart.

# Sacrament

She gave her body for my meat,
Her soul to be my wine,
And prayed that I be made complete
In sunlight and starshine.

With such abandoned grace she gave
Of all that passion taught her,
She never knew her tidal wave
Cast bread on stagnant water.

# Bread and Wine

From death of star to new star's birth,
This ache of limb, this throb of head,
This sweaty shop, this smell of earth,
For this we pray, "Give daily bread."

Then tenuous with dreams the night,
The feel of soft brown hands in mine,
Strength from your lips for one more fight:
Bread's not so dry when dipped in wine.

# Spring Reminiscence

"My sweet," you sang, and, "Sweet," I sang,
And sweet we sang together,
Glad to be young as the world was young,
Two colts too strong for a tether.

Shall ever a spring be like that spring,
Or apple blossoms as white;
Or ever clover smell like the clover
We lay upon that night?

Shall ever your hand lie in my hand,
Pulsing to it, I wonder;
Or have the gods, being jealous gods,
Envied us our thunder?

VARIA

# SUICIDE CHANT

I am the seed
The Sower sowed;
I am the deed
His hand bestowed
Upon the world.

Censure me not
If a rank weed flood
The garden plot,
Instead of a bud
To be unfurled.

Bridle your blame
If the deed prove less
Than the bruited fame
With which it came
From nothingness.

The seed of a weed
Cannot be flowered,
Nor a hero's deed
Spring from a coward.

Pull up the weed;
Bring plow and mower;
Then fetch new seed
For the hand of the Sower.

# She of the Dancing Feet Sings

## (To Ottie Graham)

"And what would I do in heaven, pray,
 Me with my dancing feet,
 And limbs like apple boughs that sway
 When the gusty rain winds beat?

And how would I thrive in a perfect place
 Where dancing would be sin,
 With not a man to love my face,
 Nor an arm to hold me in?

The seraphs and the cherubim
 Would be too proud to bend
 To sing the faery tunes that brim
 My heart from end to end.

The wistful angels down in hell
 Will smile to see my face,
 And understand, because they fell
 From that all-perfect place."

# Judas Iscariot

I Think when Judas' mother heard
His first faint cry the night
That he was born, that worship stirred
Her at the sound and sight.
She thought his was as fair a frame
As flesh and blood had worn;
I think she made this lovely name

For him—"Star of my morn."
As any mother's son he grew
From spring to crimson spring;
I think his eyes were black, or blue,
His hair curled like a ring.
His mother's heart-strings were a lute
Whereon he all day played;
She listened rapt, abandoned, mute,
To every note he made.

I think he knew the growing Christ,
And played with Mary's son,
And where mere mortal craft sufficed,
There Judas may have won.

Perhaps he little cared or knew,
So folly-wise is youth,
That He whose hand his hand clung to
Was flesh-embodied Truth;

Until one day he heard young Christ,
With far-off eyes agleam,
Tell of a mystic, solemn tryst
Between Him and a dream.
And Judas listened, wonder-eyed,
Until the Christ was through,
Then said, "And I, though good betide,
Or ill, will go with you."

And so he followed, heard Christ preach,
Saw how by miracle
The blind man saw, the dumb got speech,
The leper found him well.
And Judas in those holy hours.
Loved Christ, and loved Him much,
And in his heart he sensed dead flowers
Bloom at the Master's touch.

And when Christ felt the death hour creep
With sullen, drunken lurch,
He said to Peter, "Feed my sheep,
And build my holy church."

He gave to each the special task
That should be his to do,
But reaching one, I hear him ask,
"What shall I give to you?"

Then Judas in his hot desire
Said, "Give me what you will."
Christ spoke to him with words of fire,
"Then, Judas, you must kill,
One whom you love, One who loves you;
As only God's son can:
This is the work for you to do
To save the creature man."

"And men to come will curse your name,
And hold you up to scorn;
In all the world will be no shame
Like yours; this is love's thorn.
It takes strong will of heart and soul,
But man is under ban.
Think, Judas, can you play this role
In heaven's mystic plan?"

So Judas took the sorry part,
Went out and spoke the word,

And gave the kiss that broke his heart,
But no one knew or heard.

And no one knew what poison ate
Into his palm that day,
Where, bright and damned, the monstrous weight
Of thirty white coins lay.

It was not death that Judas found
Upon a kindly tree;
The man was dead long ere he bound
His throat 'as final fee.
And who can say if on that day
When gates of pearl swung wide,
Christ did not go His honored way
With Judas by His side?

I think somewhere a table round
Owns Jesus as its head,
And there the saintly twelve are found
Who followed where He led.
And Judas sits down with the rest,
And none shrinks from His hand,
For there the worst is as the best,
And there they understand.

And you may think of Judas, friend,
As one who broke his word,
Whose neck came to a bitter end
For giving up his Lord.
But I would rather think of him
As the little Jewish lad
Who gave young Christ heart, soul, and limb,
And all the love he had.

# The Wise

### (For Alain Locke)

Dead men are wisest, for they know
How far the roots of flowers go,
How long a seed must rot to grow.

Dead men alone bear frost and rain
On throbless heart and heatless brain,
And feel no stir of joy or pain.

Dead men alone are satiate;
They sleep and dream and have no weight,
To curb their rest, of love or hate.

Strange, men should flee their company,
Or think me strange who long to be
Wrapped in their cool immunity.

# MARY, MOTHER OF CHRIST

That night she felt those searching hands
Grip deep upon her breast,
She laughed and sang a silly tune
To lull her babe to rest;

That night she kissed his coral lips
How could she know the rest?

# DIALOGUE

SOUL: There is no stronger thing than song;
    In sun and rain and leafy trees
    It wafts the timid soul along
    On crested waves of melodies.

BODY: But leaves the body bare to feed
    Its hunger with its very need.

SOUL: Although the frenzied belly writhes,
    Yet render up in song your tithes;
    Song is the weakling's oaken rod,
    His Jacob's ladder dropped from God.

BODY: Song is not drink; song is not meat,
    Nor strong, thick shoes for naked feet.

SOUL: Who sings by unseen hands is fed
    With honeyed milk and warm, white bread;
    His ways in pastures green are led,
    And perfumed oil illumes his head;
    His cup with wine is surfeited,
    And when the last low note is read,
    He sings among the lipless dead
    With singing stars to crown his head.

BODY: But will song buy a wooden box
    The length of me from toe to crown,
    To keep me safe from carrion flocks
    When singing's done and lyre laid down?

# In Memory of Col. Charles Young

Along the shore the tall, thin grass
That fringes that dark river,
While sinuously soft feet pass,
Begins to bleed and quiver.

The great dark voice breaks with a sob
Across the womb of night;
Above your grave the tom-toms throb,
And the hills are weird with light.

The great dark heart is like a well
Drained bitter by the sky,
And all the honeyed lies they tell
Come there to thirst and die.

No lie is strong enough to kill
The roots that work below;
From your rich dust and slaughtered will
A tree with tongues will grow.

# To My Friends

You feeble few that hold me somewhat more
Than all I am; base clay and spittle joined
To shape an aimless whim substantial; coined
Amiss one idle hour, this heart, though
poor,—
O golden host I count upon the ends
Of one bare hand, with fingers still to
spare,—
Is rich enough for this: to harbor there
In opulence its frugal meed of friends.
Let neither lose his faith, lest by such loss
Each find insufferable his daily cross.
And be not less immovable to me,
Not less love-leal and staunch, than my heart is.
In brief, these fine heroics come to this,
My friends: if you are true, I needs must be.

# Gods

I Fast and pray and go to church,
And put my penny in,
But God's not fooled by such slight tricks,
And I'm not saved from sin.

I cannot hide from Him the gods
That revel in my heart,
Nor can I find an easy word
To tell them to depart:

God's alabaster turrets gleam
Too high for me to win,
Unless He turns His face and lets
Me bring my own gods in.

# To John Keats, Poet. At Spring Time*

## (For Carl Van Vechten)

I Cannot hold my peace, John Keats;
There never was a spring like this;
It is an echo, that repeats
My last year's song and next year's bliss.
I know, in spite of all men say
Of Beauty, you have felt her most.
Yea, even in your grave her way
Is laid. Poor, troubled, lyric ghost,
Spring never was so fair and dear
As Beauty makes her seem this year.

I cannot hold my peace, John Keats,
I am as helpless in the toil
Of Spring as any lamb that bleats
To feel the solid earth recoil
Beneath his puny legs. Spring beats
Her tocsin call to those who love her,
And lo! the dogwood petals cover

Her breast with drifts of snow, and sleek
White gulls fly screaming to her, and hover
About her shoulders, and kiss her cheek,
While white and purple lilacs muster
A strength that bears them to a cluster
Of color and odor; for her sake
All things that slept are now awake.

And you and I, shall we lie still,
John Keats, while Beauty summons us?
Somehow I feel your sensitive will
Is pulsing up some tremulous
Sap road of a maple tree, whose leaves

---

* Spring, 1924.

Grow music as they grow, since your
Wild voice is in them, a harp that grieves
For life that opens death's dark door.
Though dust, your fingers still can push
The Vision Splendid to a birth,
Though now they work as grass in the hushi
Of the night on the broad sweet page of the earth.
"John Keats is dead," they say, but I
Who hear your full insistent cry
In bud and blossom, leaf and tree,
Know John Keats still writes poetry.

And while my head is earthward bowed
To read new life sprung from your shroud,
Folks seeing me must think it strange
That merely spring should so derange
My mind. They do not know that you,
John Keats, keep revel with me, too.

# On Going

### (For Willard Johnson)

A Grave is all too weak a thing
To hold my fancy long;
I'll bear a blossom with the spring,
Or be a blackbird's song,

I think that I shall fade with ease,
Melt into earth like snow,
Be food for hungry, growing trees,
Or help the lilies blow.

And if my love should lonely walk,
Quite of my nearness fain,
I may come back to her, and talk
In liquid words of rain.

# HARSH WORLD THAT LASHEST ME

## (For Walter White)

Harsh World that lashest me each day,
Dub me not cowardly because
I seem to find no sudden way
To throttle you or clip your claws.
No force compels me to the wound
Whereof my body bears the scar;
Although my feet are on the ground,
Doubt not my eyes are on a star.

You cannot keep me captive, World,
Entrammeled, chained, spit on, and spurned.
More free than all your flags unfurled,
I give my body to be burned.
I mount my cross because I will,
I drink the hemlock which you give
For wine which you withhold-and still,
Because I will not die, I live.
I live because an ember in
Me smoulders to regain its fire,
Because what is and what has been
Not yet have conquered my desire.
I live to prove the groping clod
Is surely more than simple dust;
I live to see the breath of God
Beatify the carnal crust.

But when I will, World, I can go,
Though triple bronze should wall me round,
Slip past your guard as swift as snow,
Translated without pain or sound.
Within myself is lodged the key
To that vast room of couches laid
For those too proud to live and see
Their dreams of light eclipsed in shade.

# Requiescam

*I am for sleeping and forgetting*
*1 All that has gone before;*
*I am for lying still and letting*
*Who will beat at my door;*
*I would my life's cold sun were setting*
*To rise for me no more.*

# A Note About the Author

Countee Cullen (1903–1946) was an American poet, novelist, and playwright. In his youth, Cullen moved frequently with his mother Elizabeth Thomas Lucas before settling in Harlem at the age of nine, where he was raised by his grandmother Amanda Porter. In 1917, following her death, he was adopted by Reverend Frederick A. Cullen of Salem Methodist Episcopal Church, who led the largest congregation in Harlem and would later become president of the local NAACP chapter. He excelled in high school, graduating with honors to enroll at NYU, where he gained a reputation as a prize-winning poet whose works appeared in *Harper's*, *Crisis*, and *Poetry*. In 1925, he went to Harvard for a masters in English just as his first collection, *Color* (1925), was published to popular and critical acclaim. He graduated in 1926, after which he published two more collections—*The Ballad of the Brown Girl* (1927) and *Copper Sun* (1927)—cementing his reputation as a leading writer of the Harlem Renaissance. Cullen was known for his friendly and professional associations with such figures as Duke Ellington, Langston Hughes, and Alain Locke, defining artists and intellectuals of their generation. Throughout his life, Cullen struggled with his sexuality and shy demeanor, pursuing relationships with men and women alike. He received a 1928 Guggenheim Fellowship, using it to write *The Black Christ and Other Poems*, a controversial collection for its comparison of the crucifixion to the lynching of Black Americans. Despite the backlash, he continued to write and publish for the next two decades, turning to plays and children's fiction at the end of his career and, at one point, mentoring a young James Baldwin. His translation of Euripides' tragedy *Medea* is considered the first of its kind by a Black American writer. Often overshadowed by his more outspoken peers, Cullen's legacy is that of a master of traditional poetic forms who used his voice and tremendous intellect to uplift and examine the lives of all African Americans.

# A Note from the Publisher

Spanning many genres, from non-fiction essays to literature classics to children's books and lyric poetry, Mint Edition books showcase the master works of our time in a modern new package. The text is freshly typeset, is clean and easy to read, and features a new note about the author in each volume. Many books also include exclusive new introductory material. Every book boasts a striking new cover, which makes it as appropriate for collecting as it is for gift giving. Mint Edition books are only printed when a reader orders them, so natural resources are not wasted. We're proud that our books are never manufactured in excess and exist only in the exact quantity they need to be read and enjoyed. To learn more and view our library, go to minteditionbooks.com

# bookfinity & MINT EDITIONS

Enjoy more of your favorite classics with Bookfinity,
a new search and discovery experience for readers.
With Bookfinity, you can discover more vintage
literature for your collection, find your Reader Type,
track books you've read or want to read,
and add reviews to your favorite books.
Visit www.bookfinity.com, and click on
Take the Quiz to get started.

Don't forget to follow us
@bookfinityofficial and @mint_editions